DANCING ANIMALS COLORING BOOK

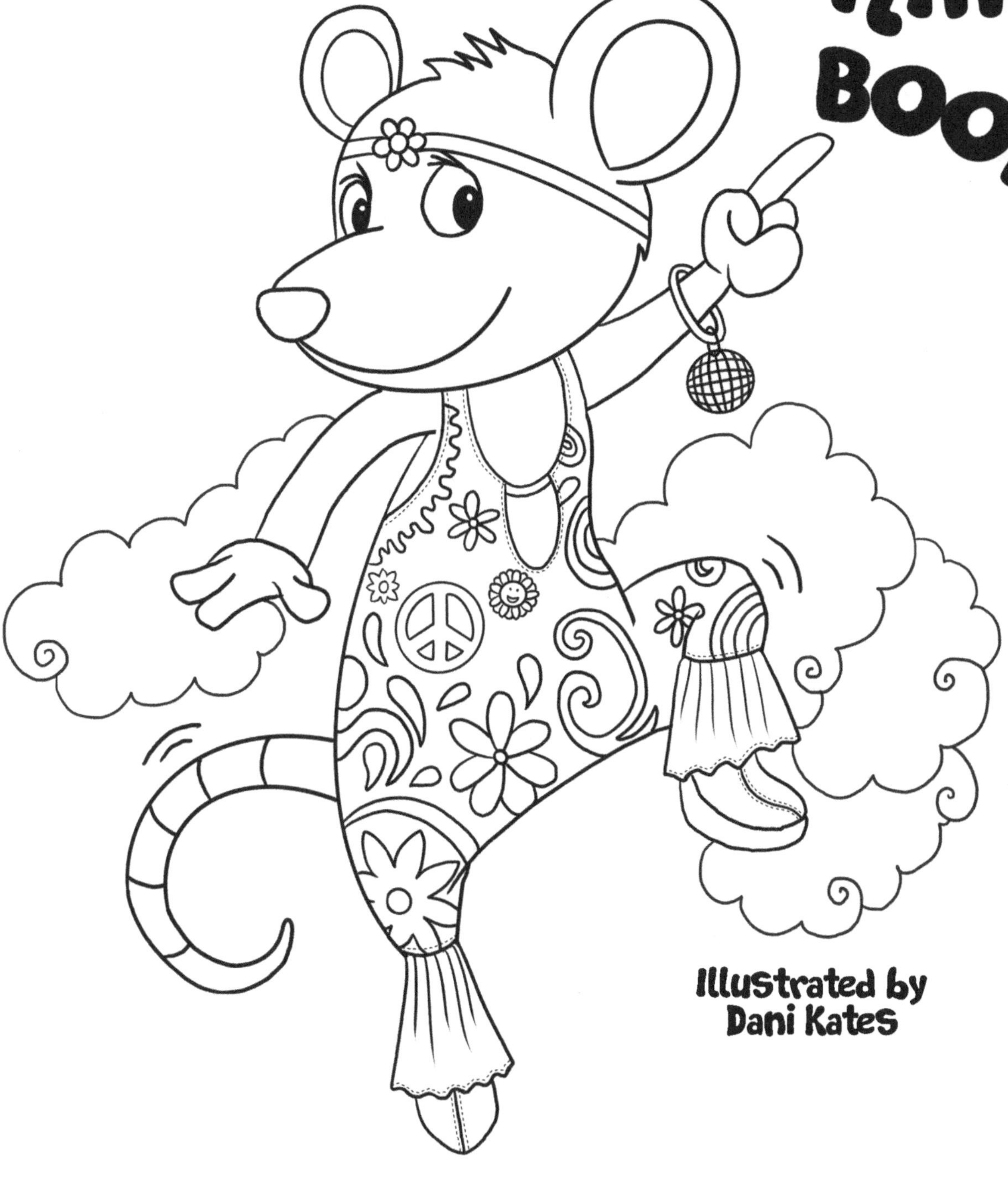

Illustrated by
Dani Kates

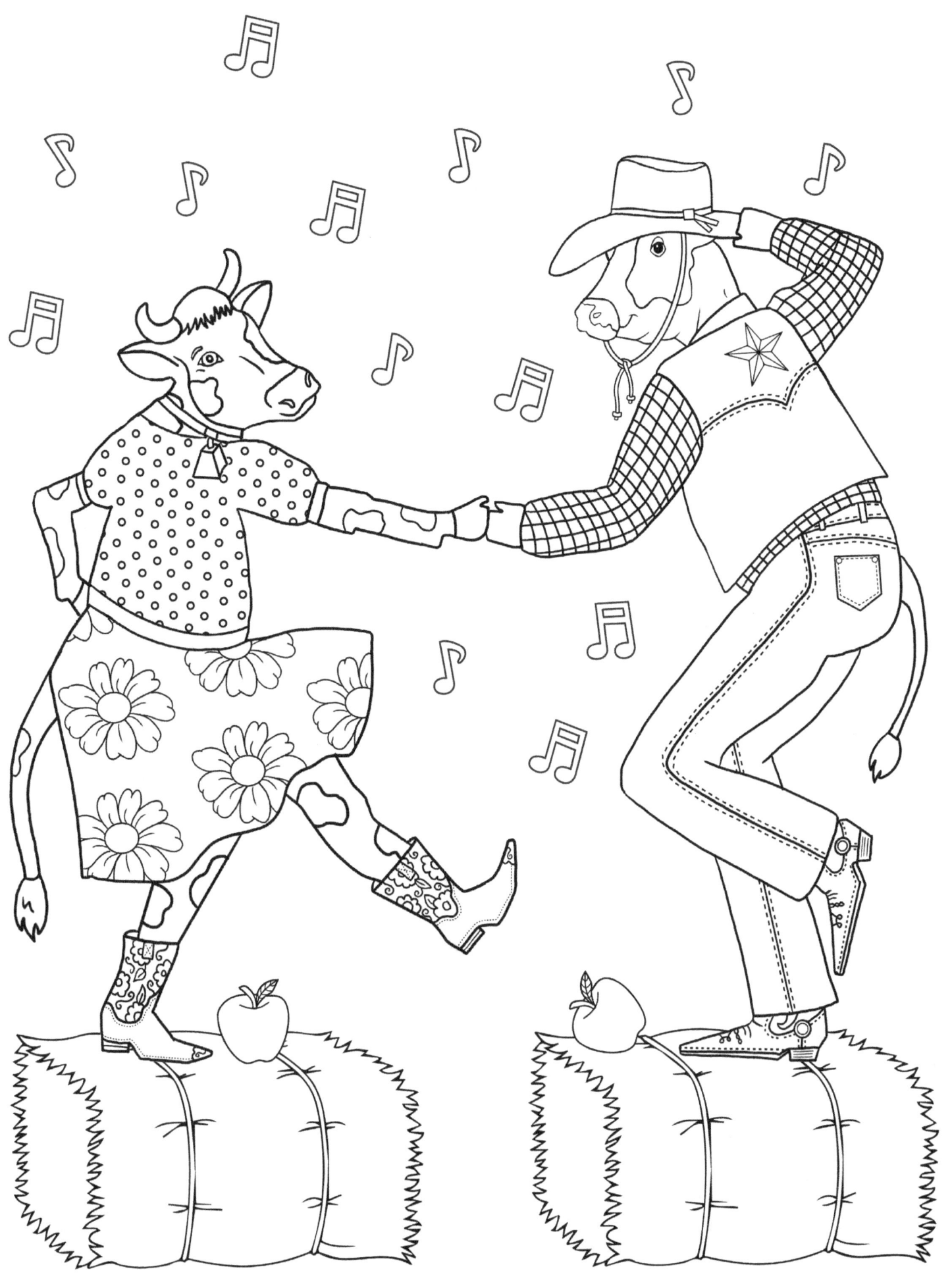

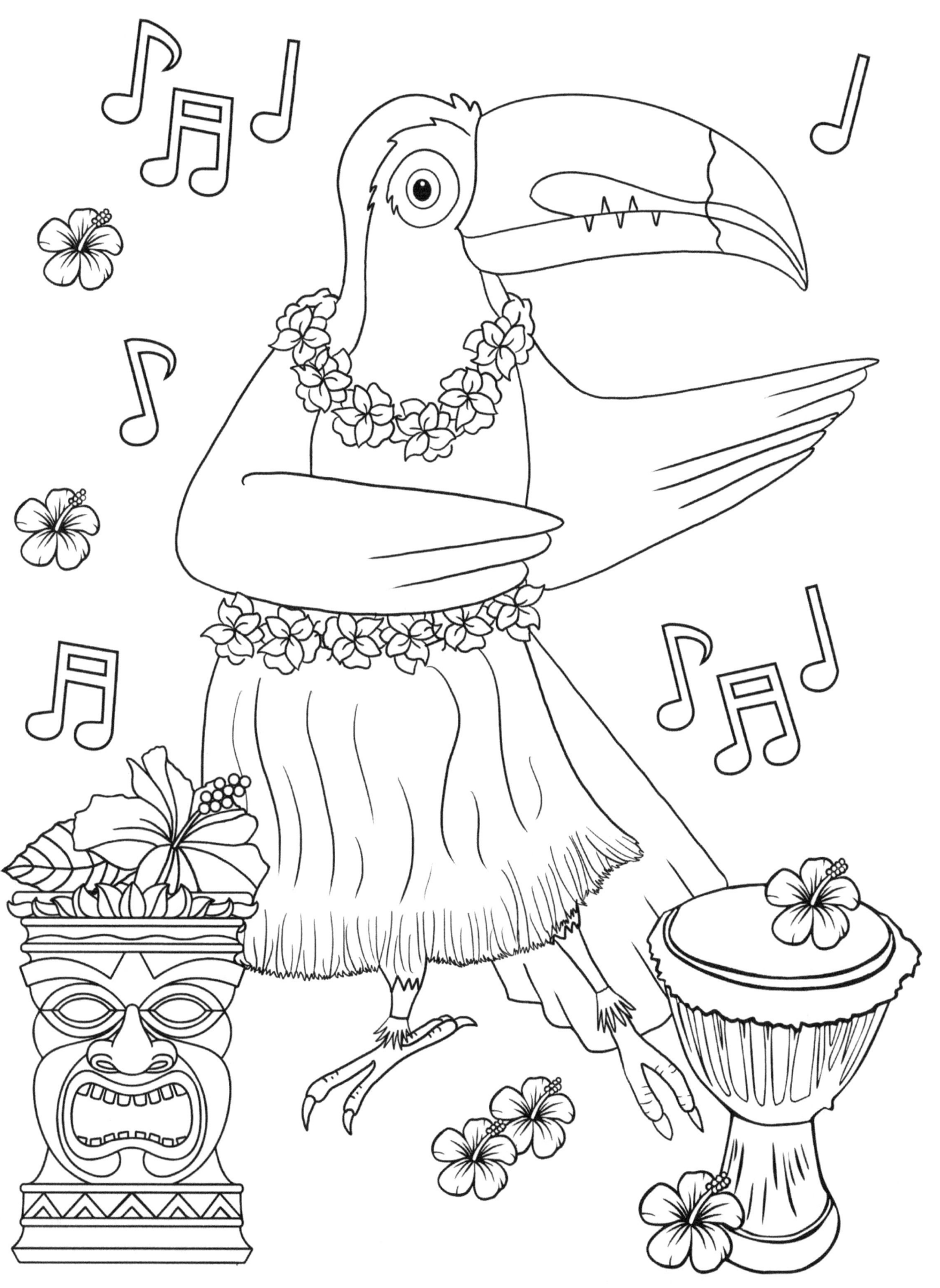

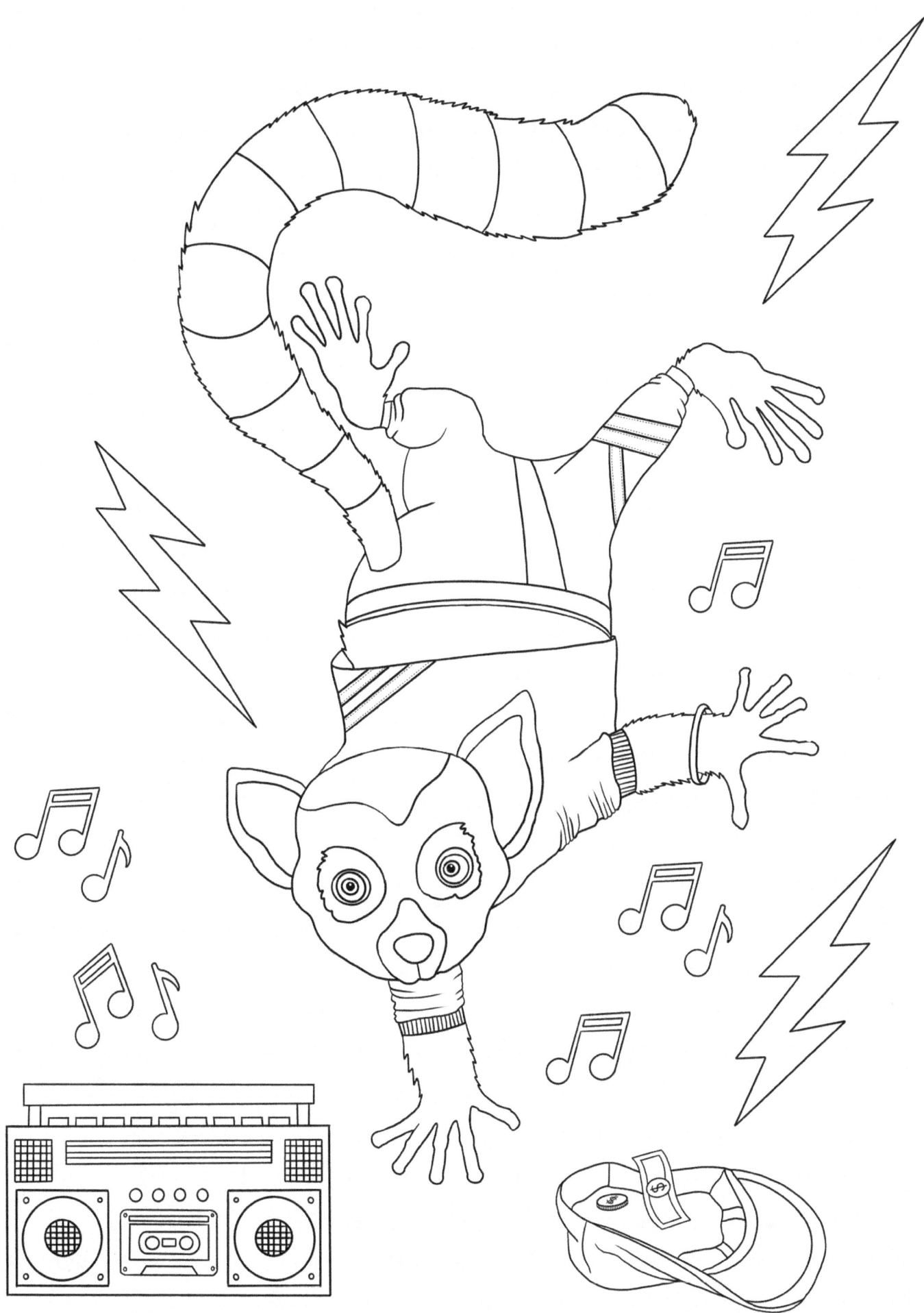

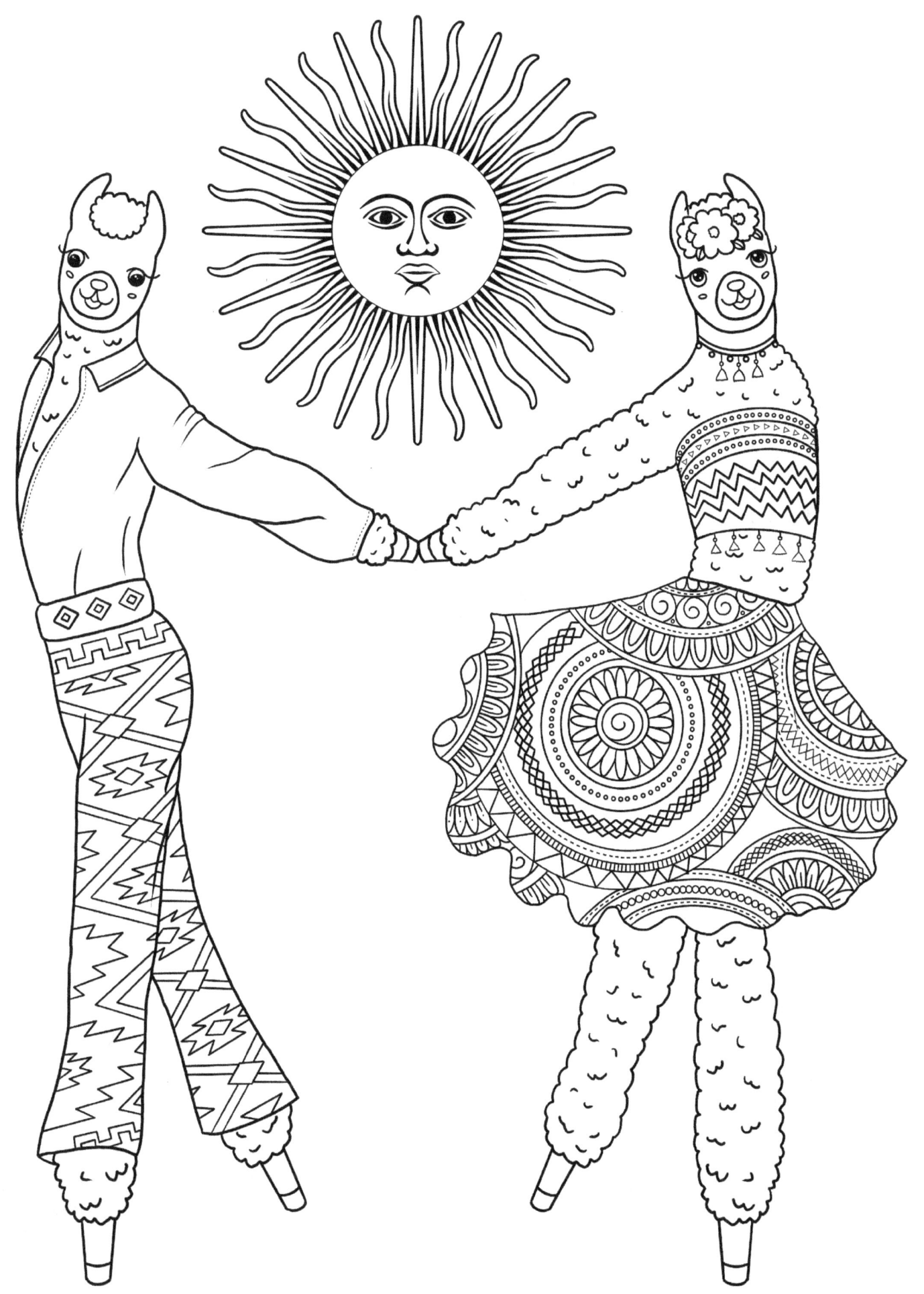

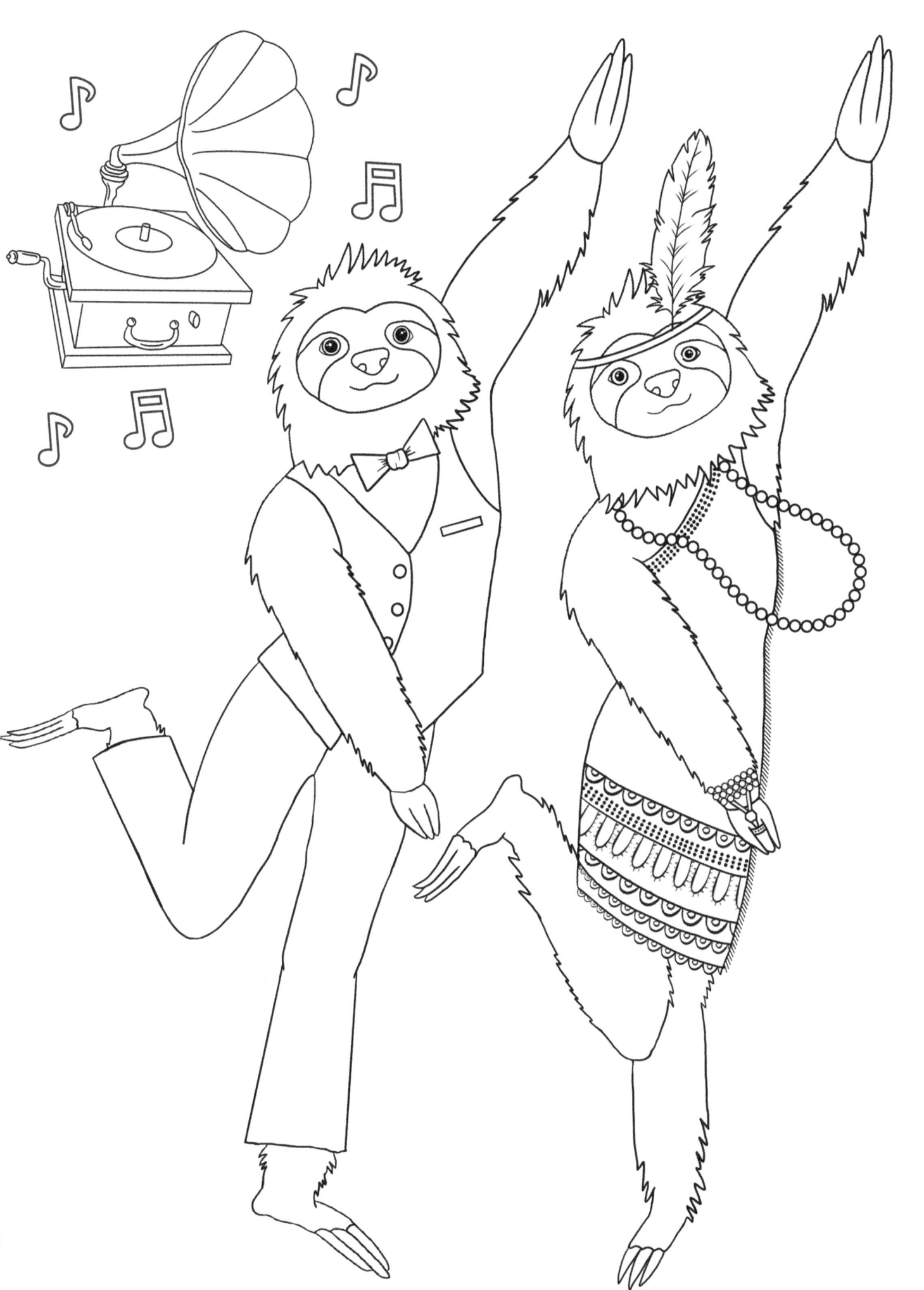

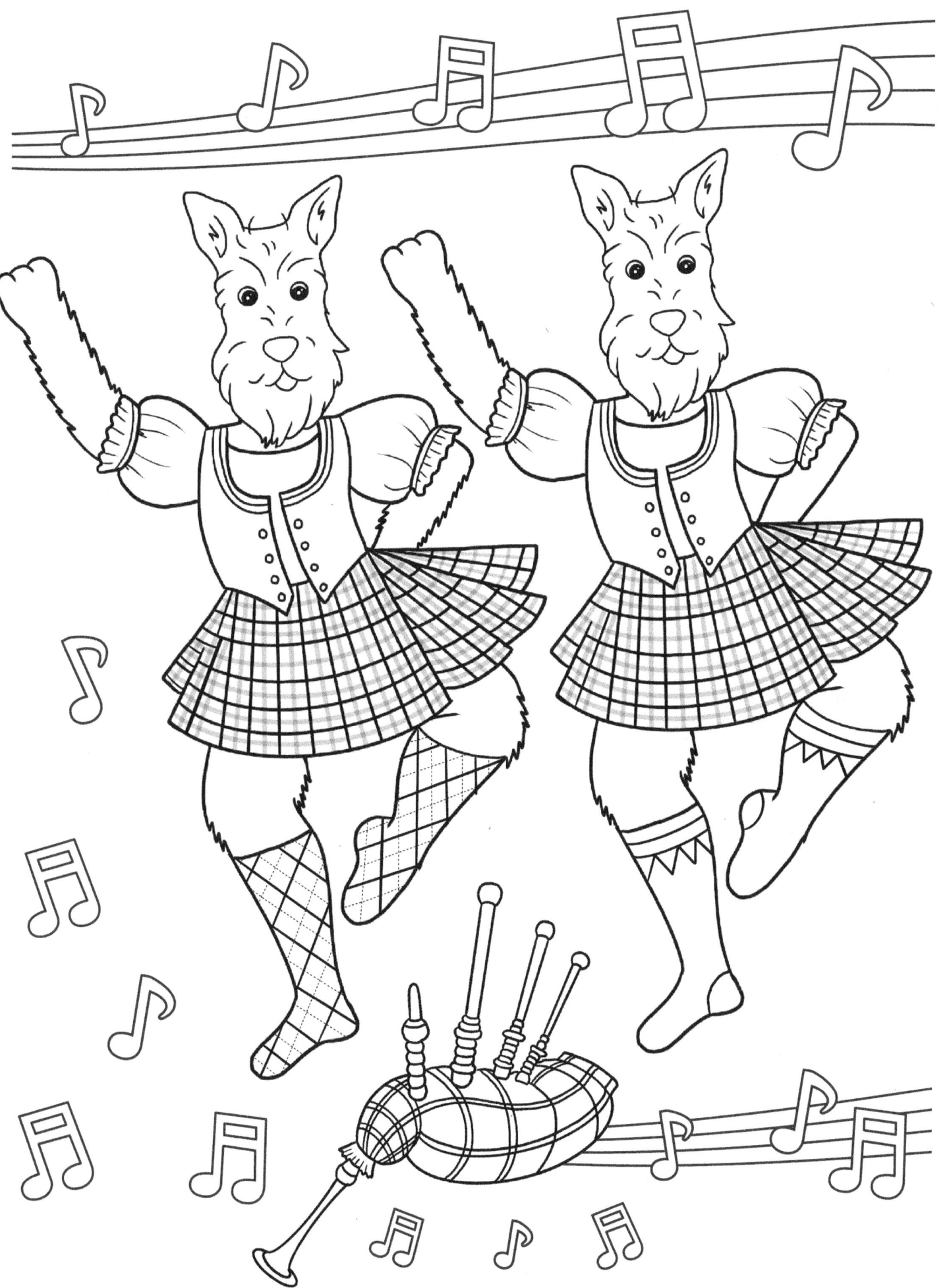

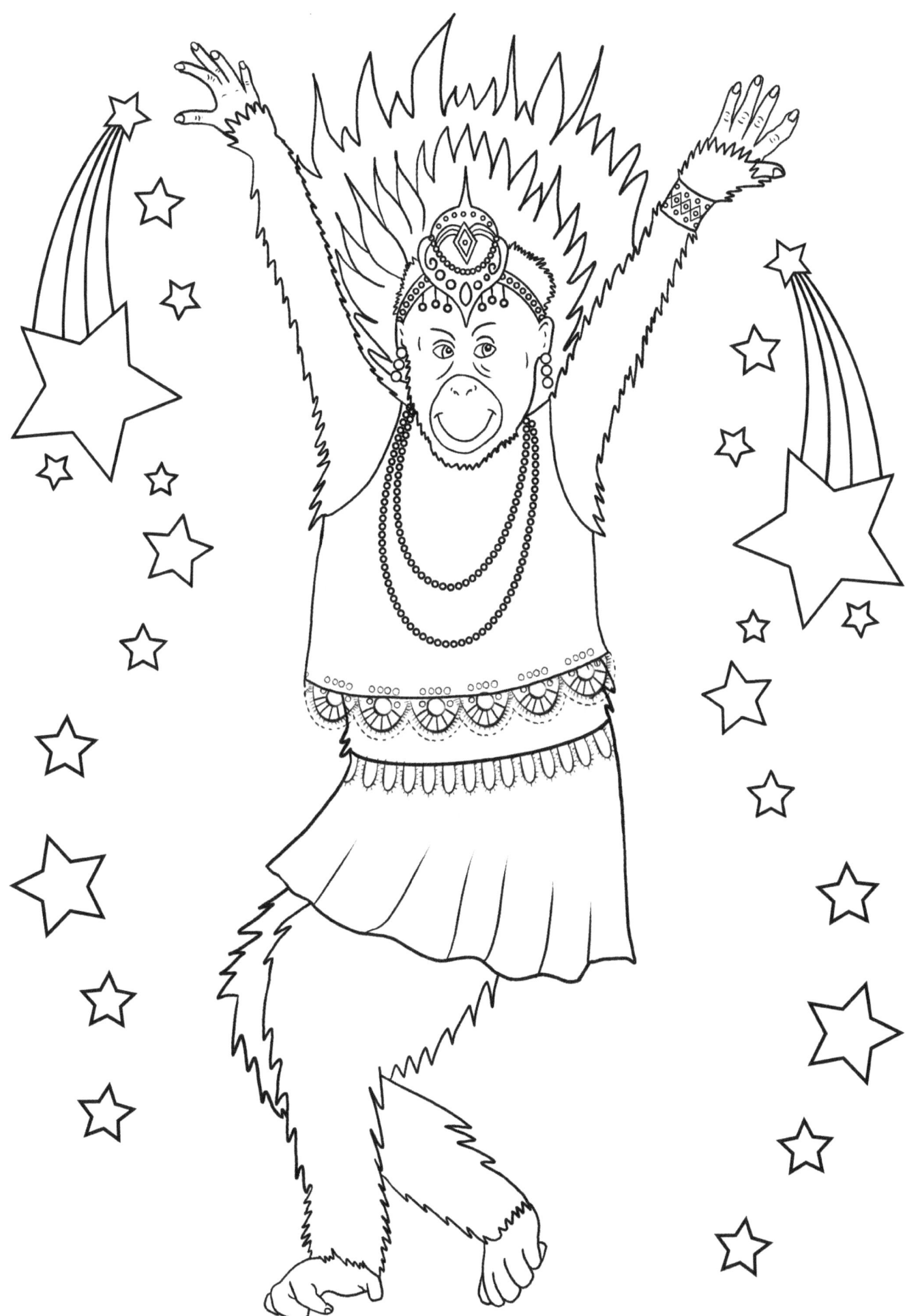

GIRLS JUST WANT TO HAVE FUN.

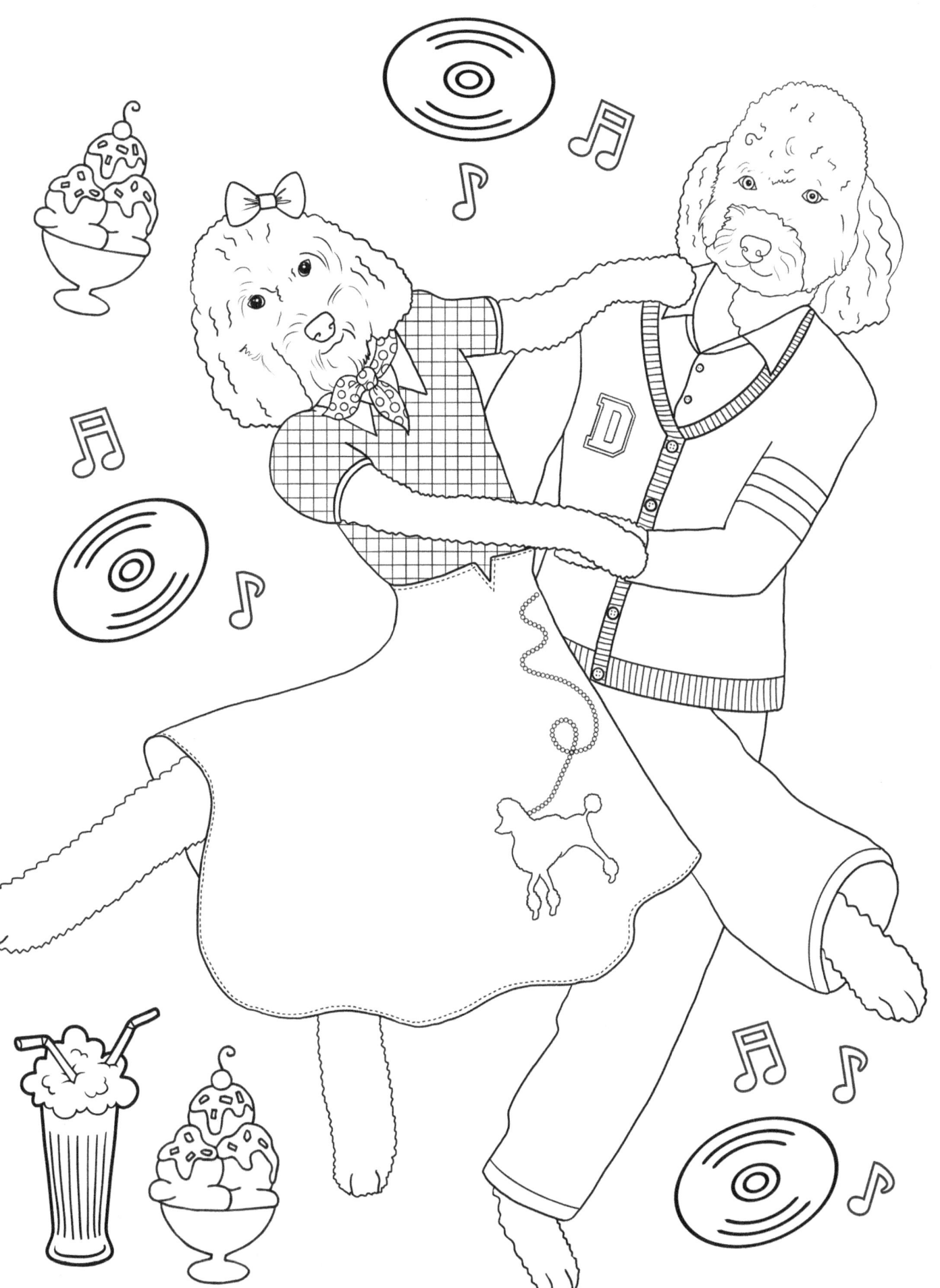

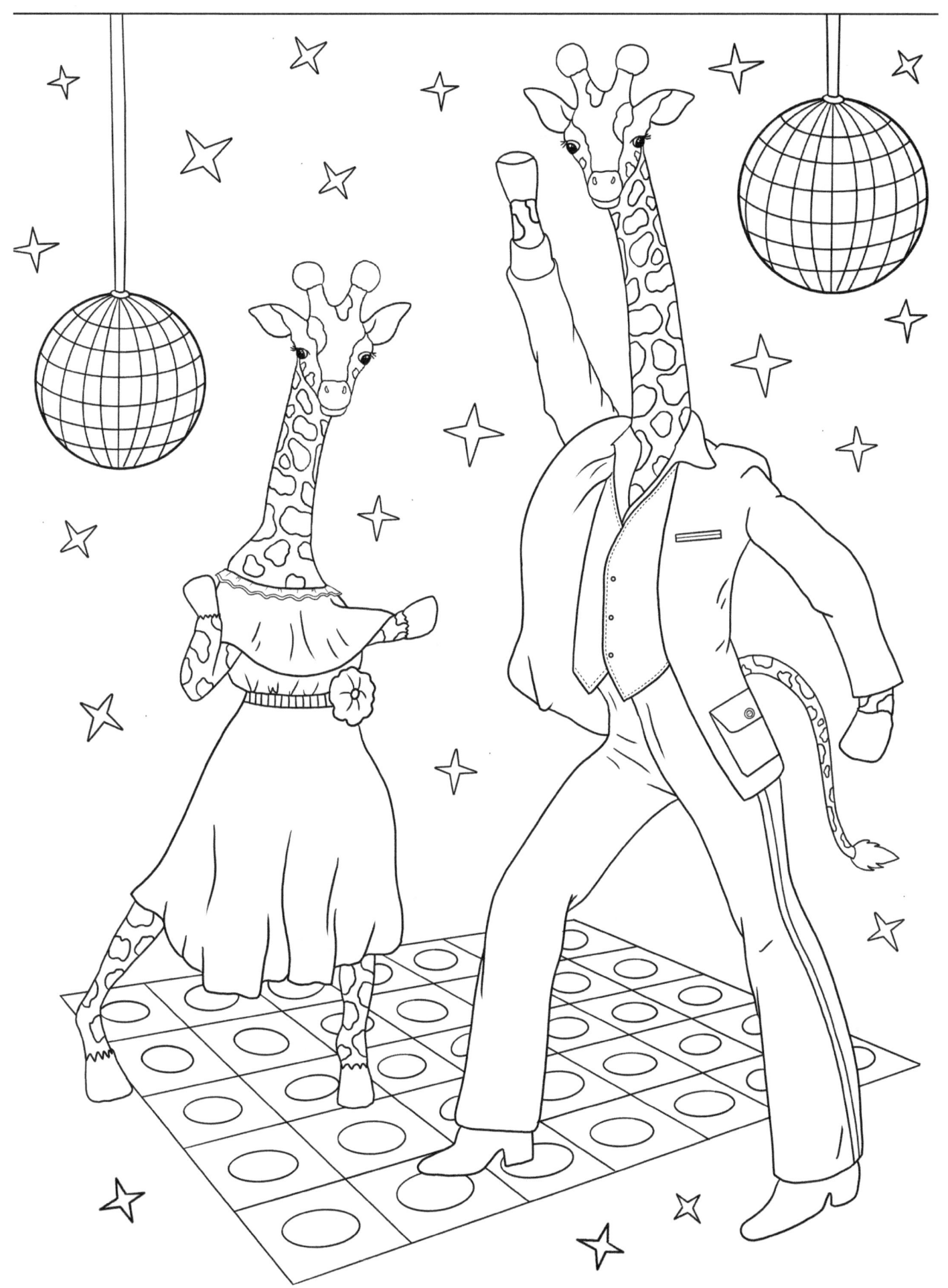

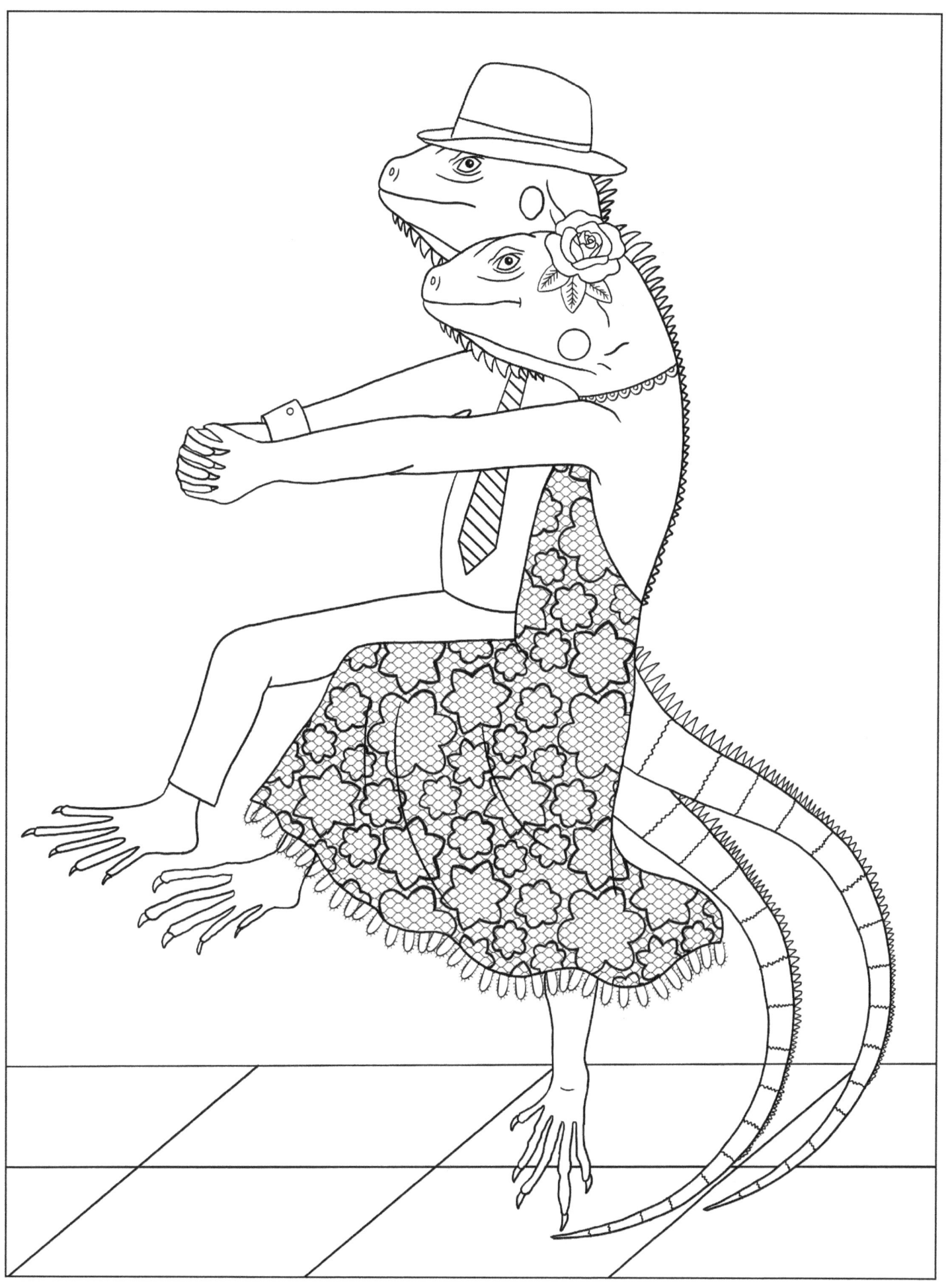

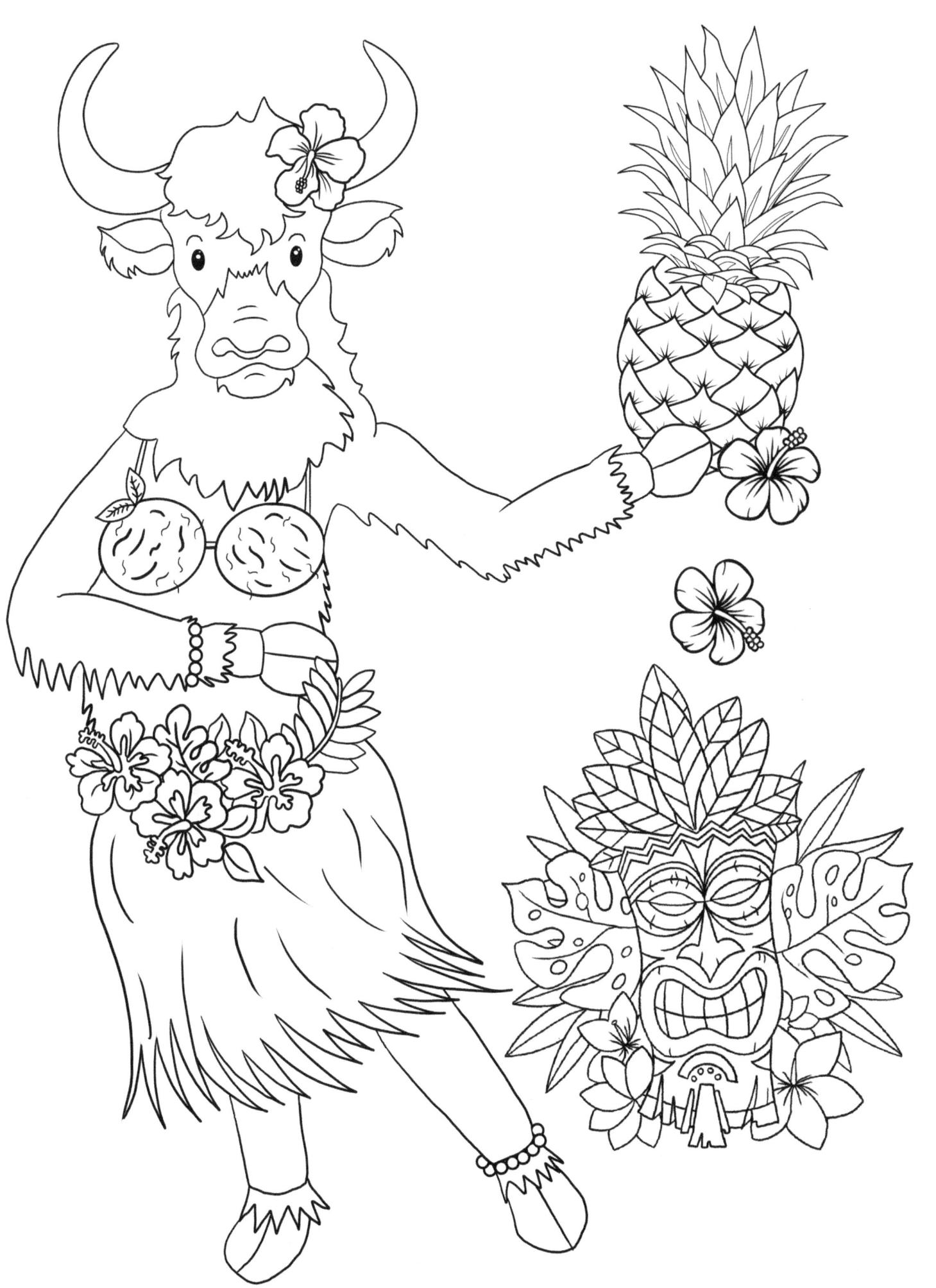

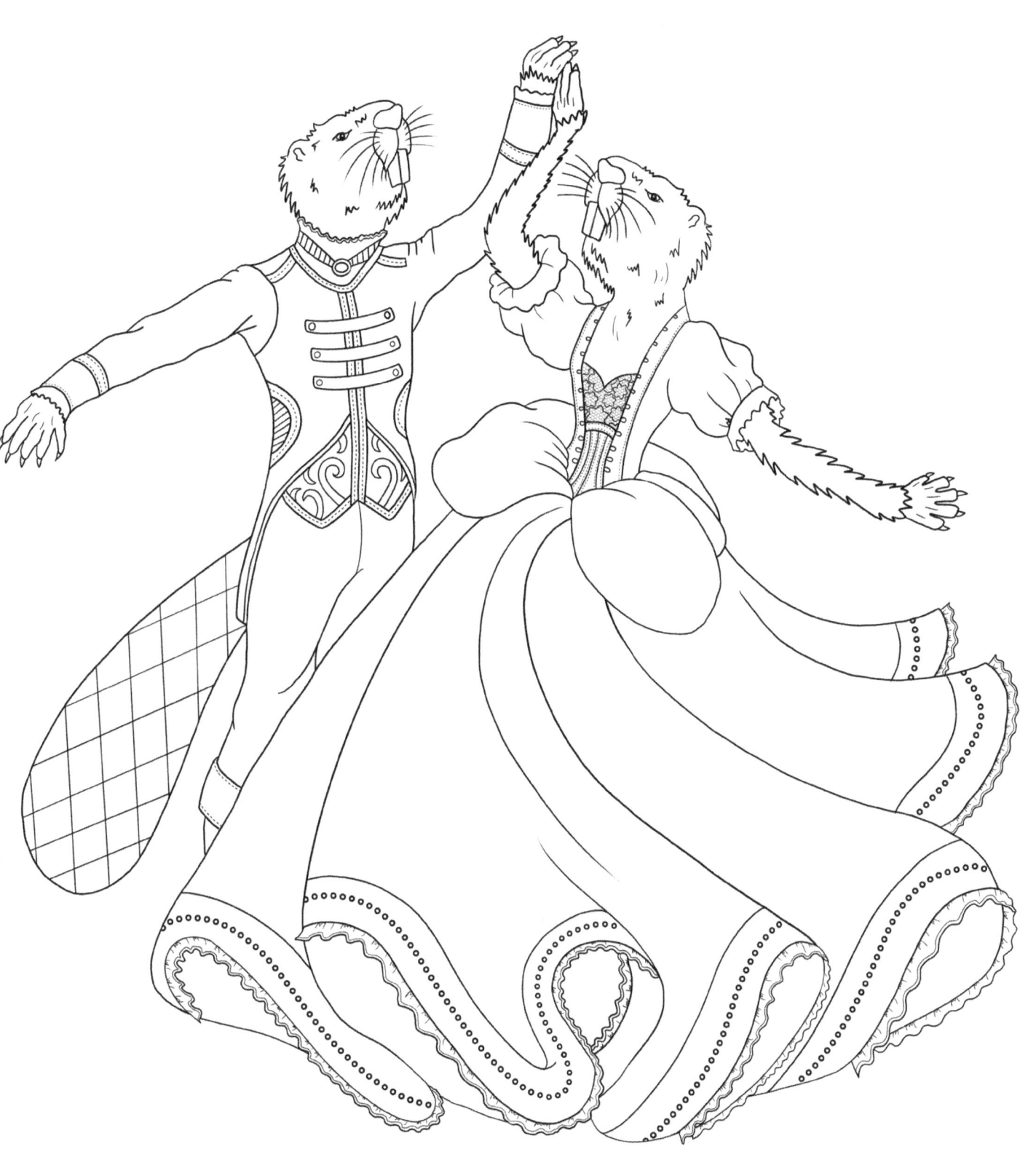

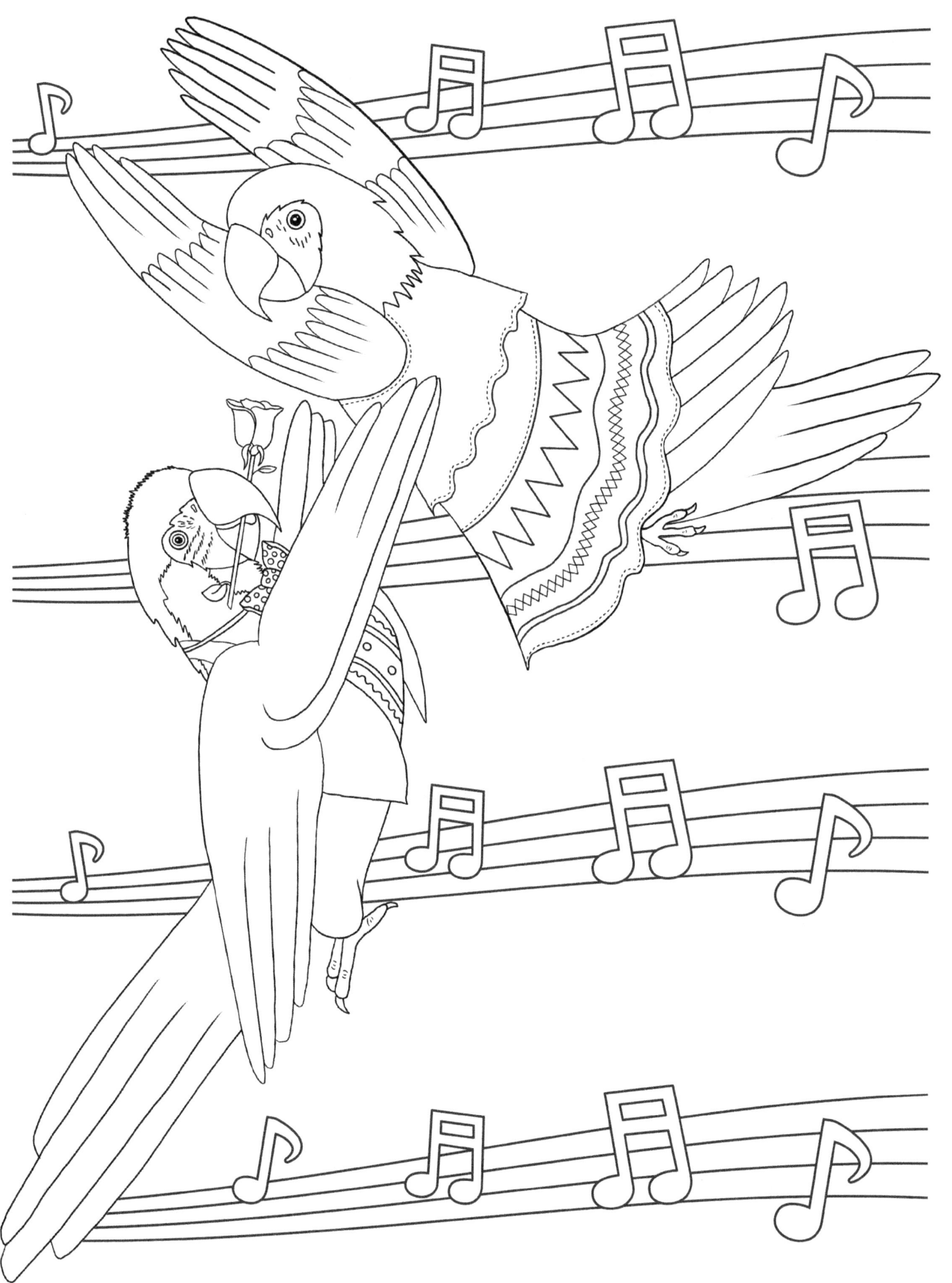

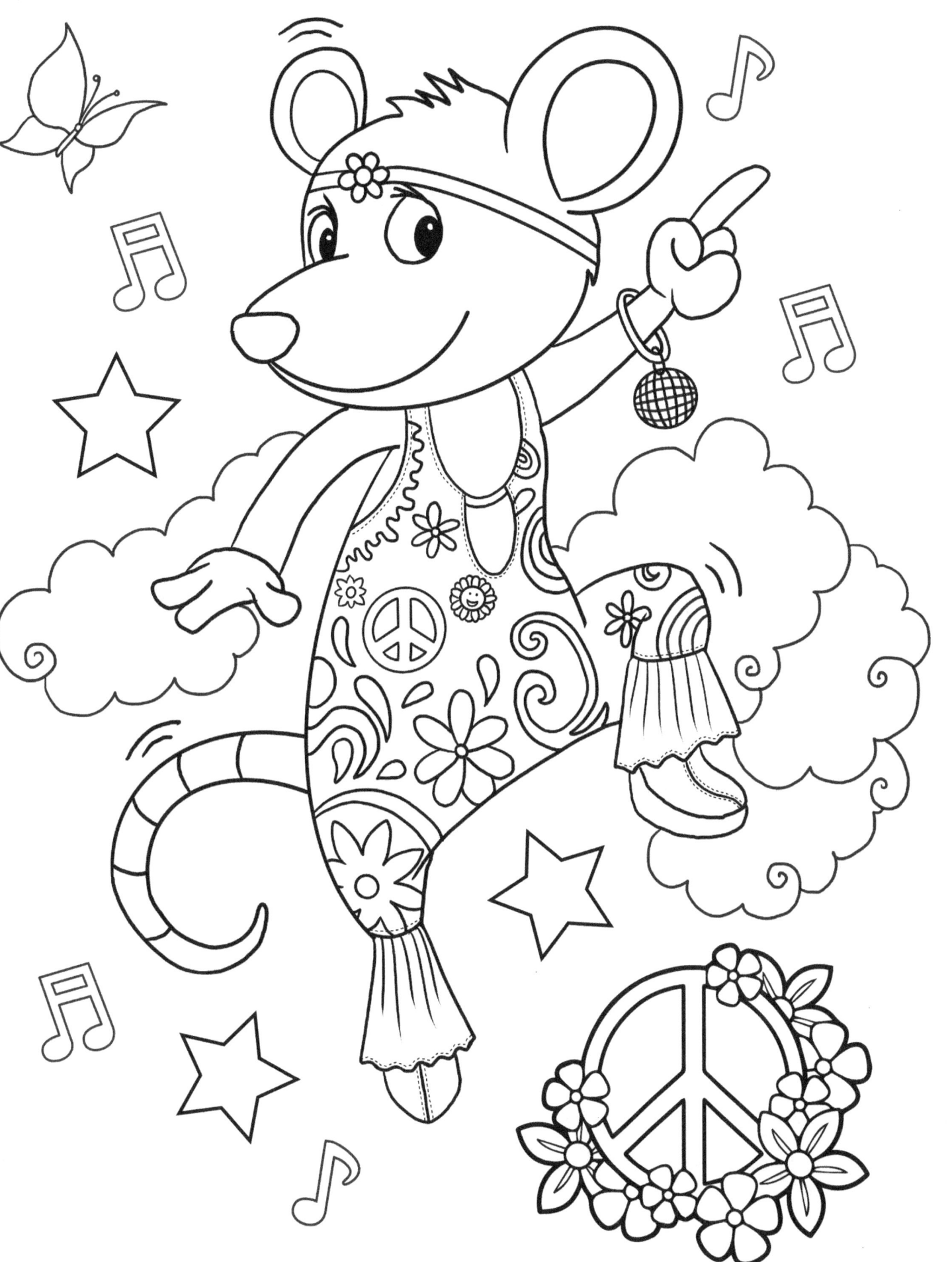

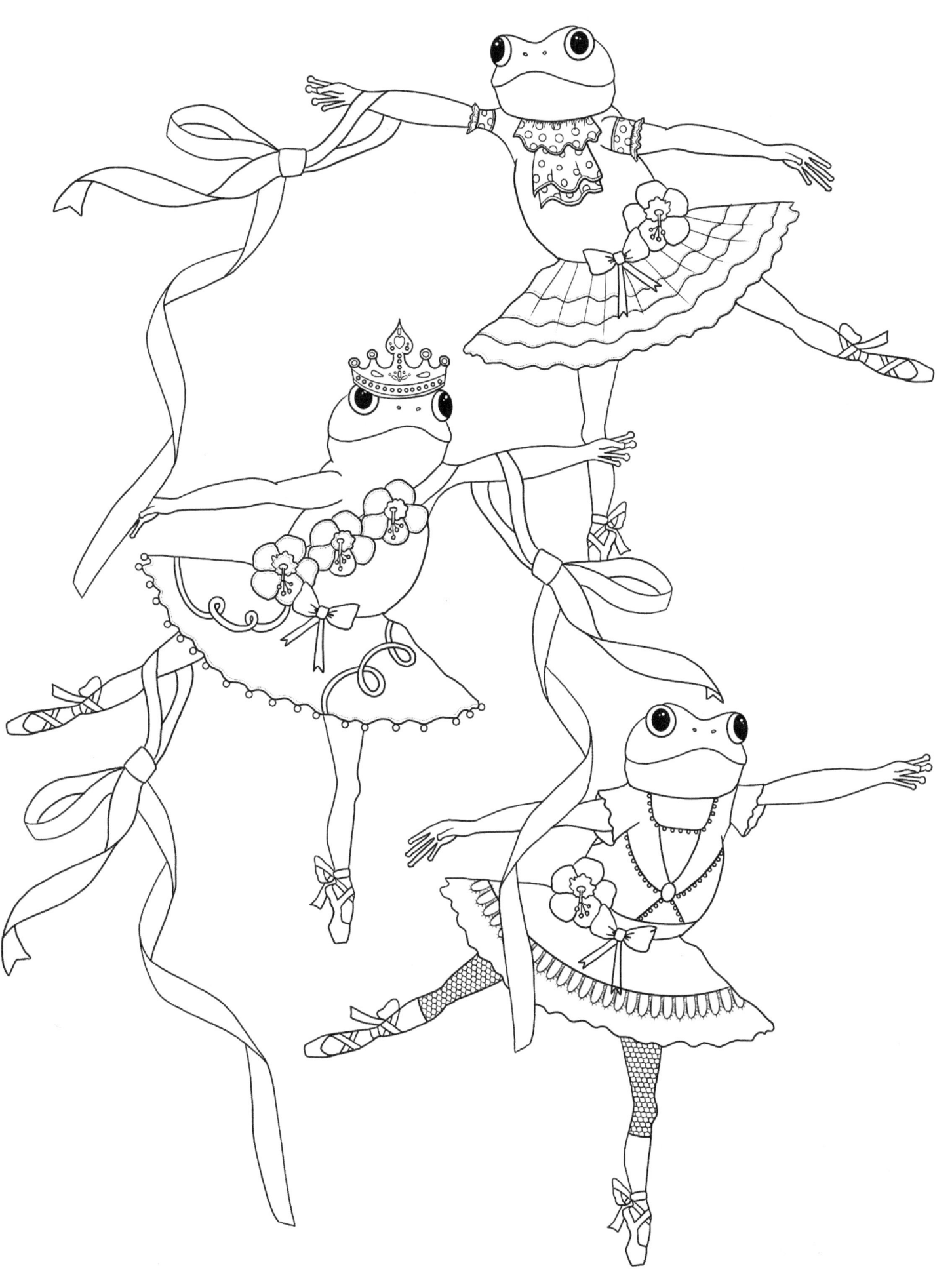

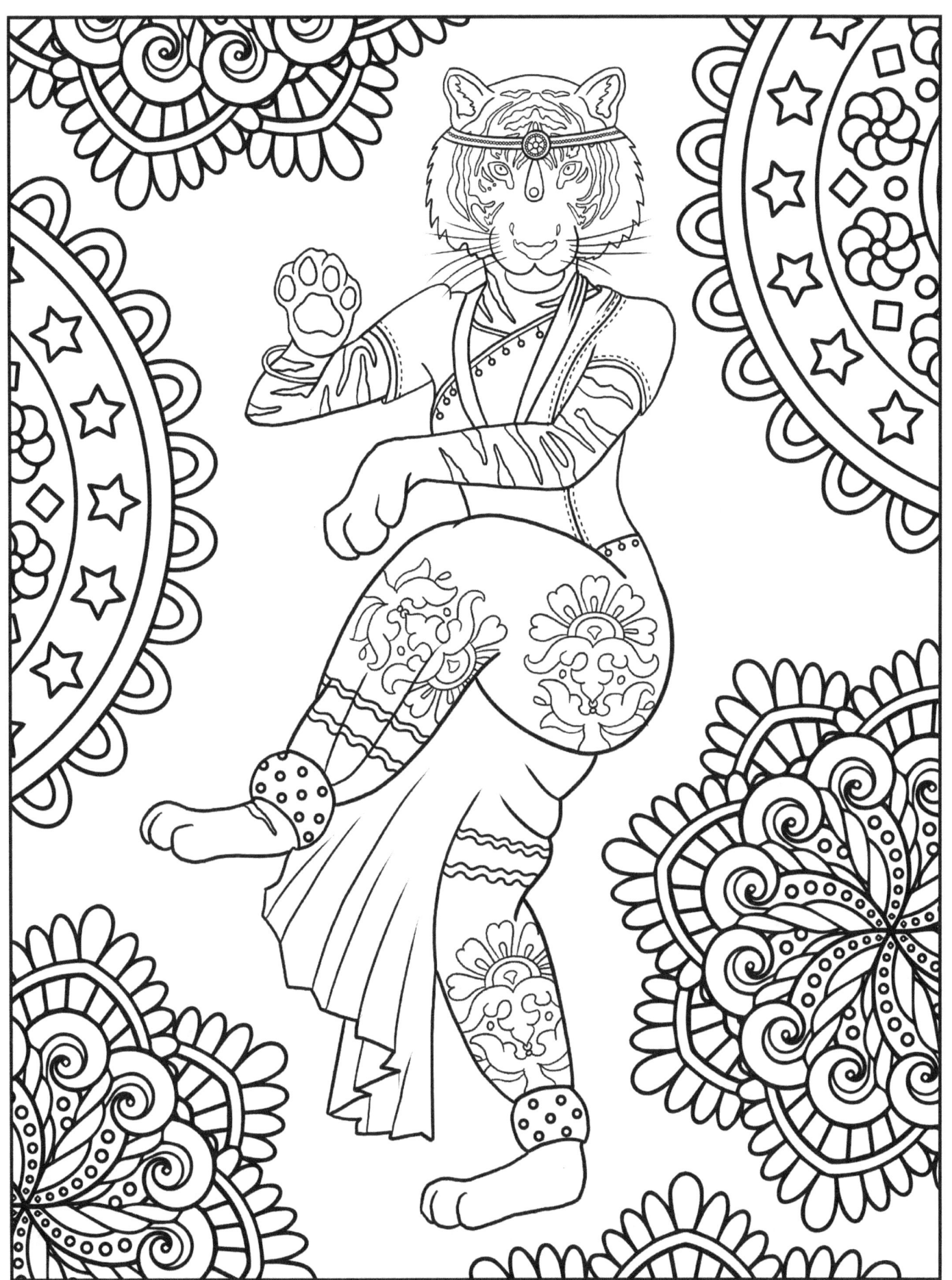

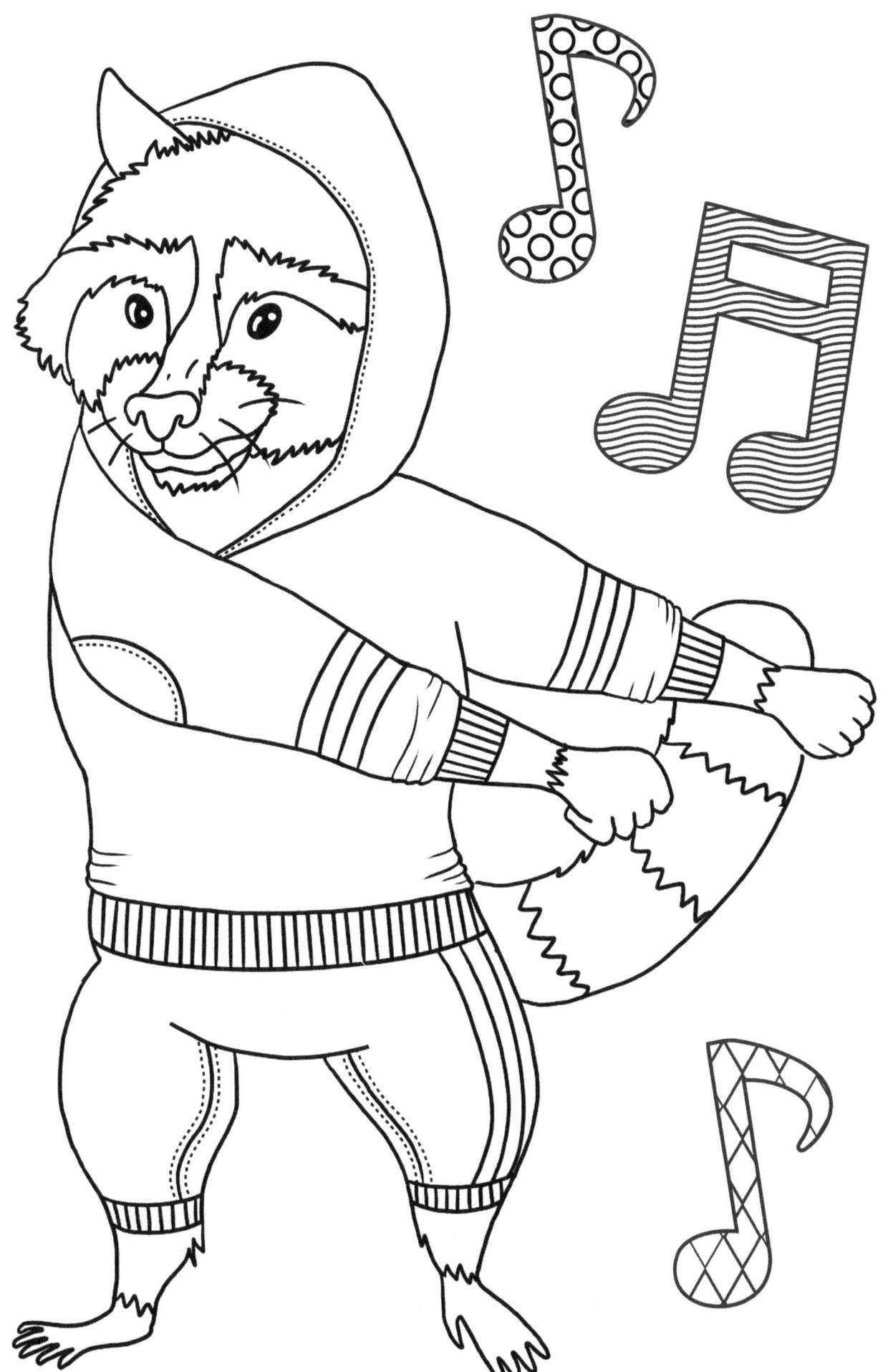

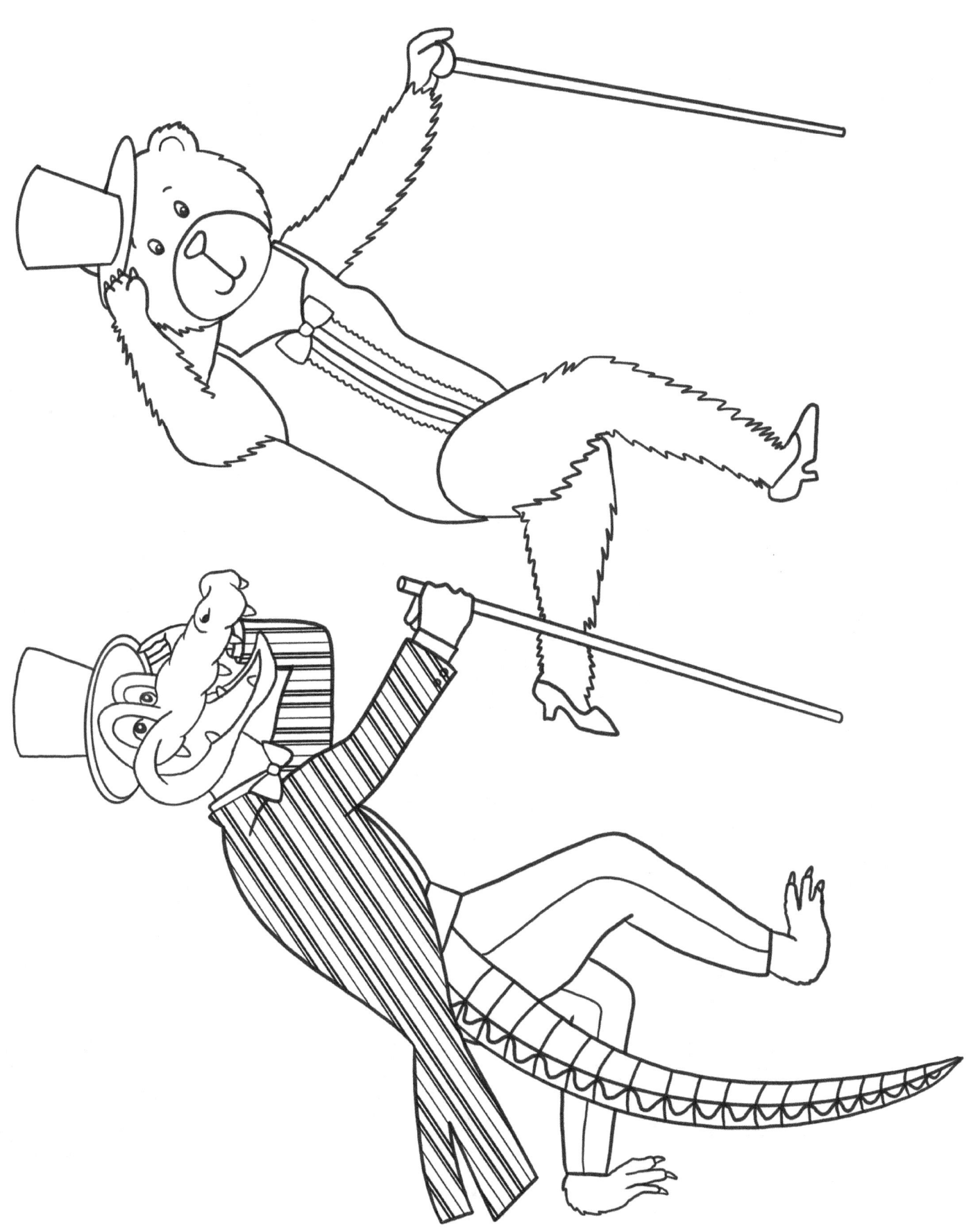

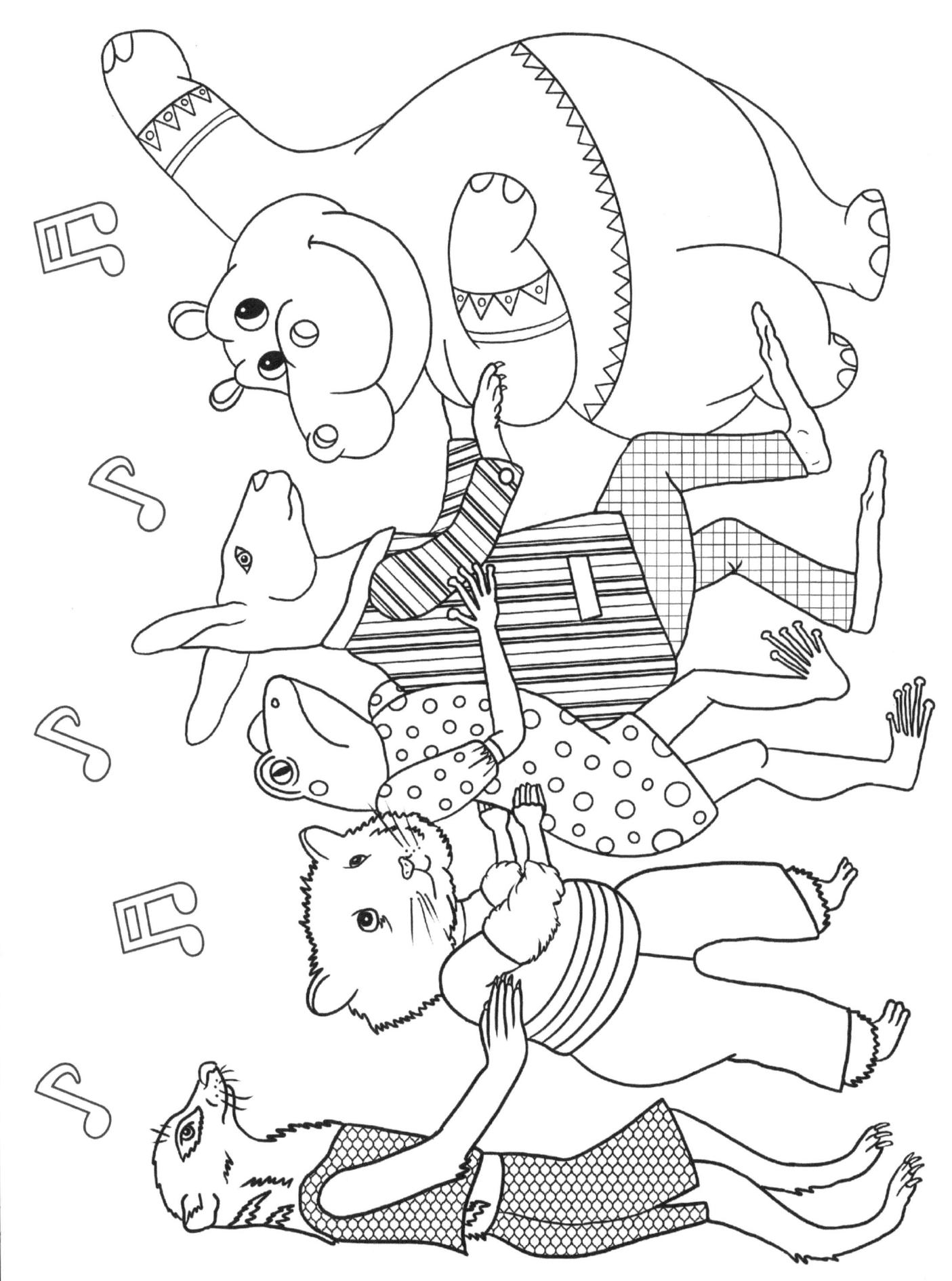

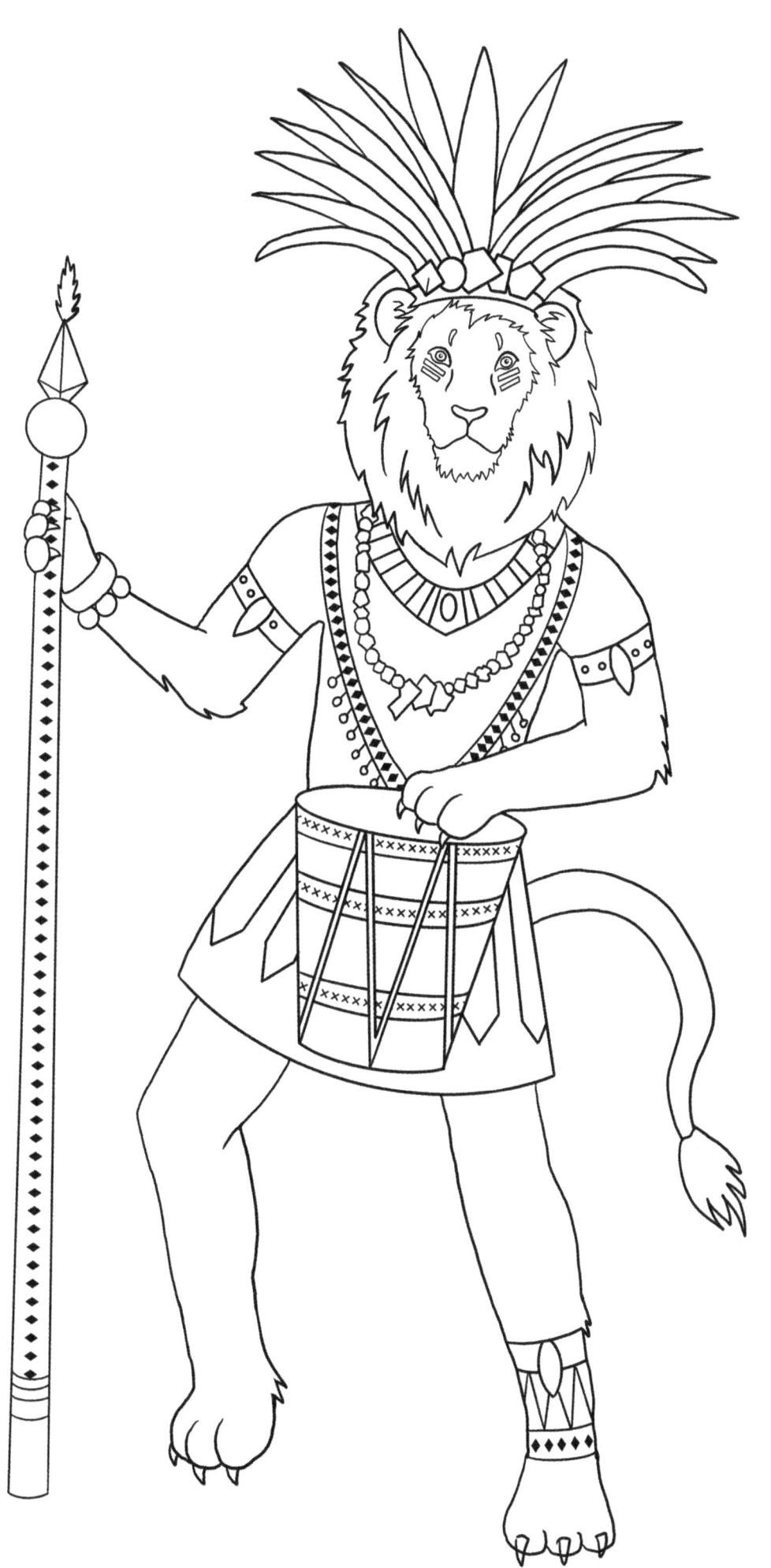

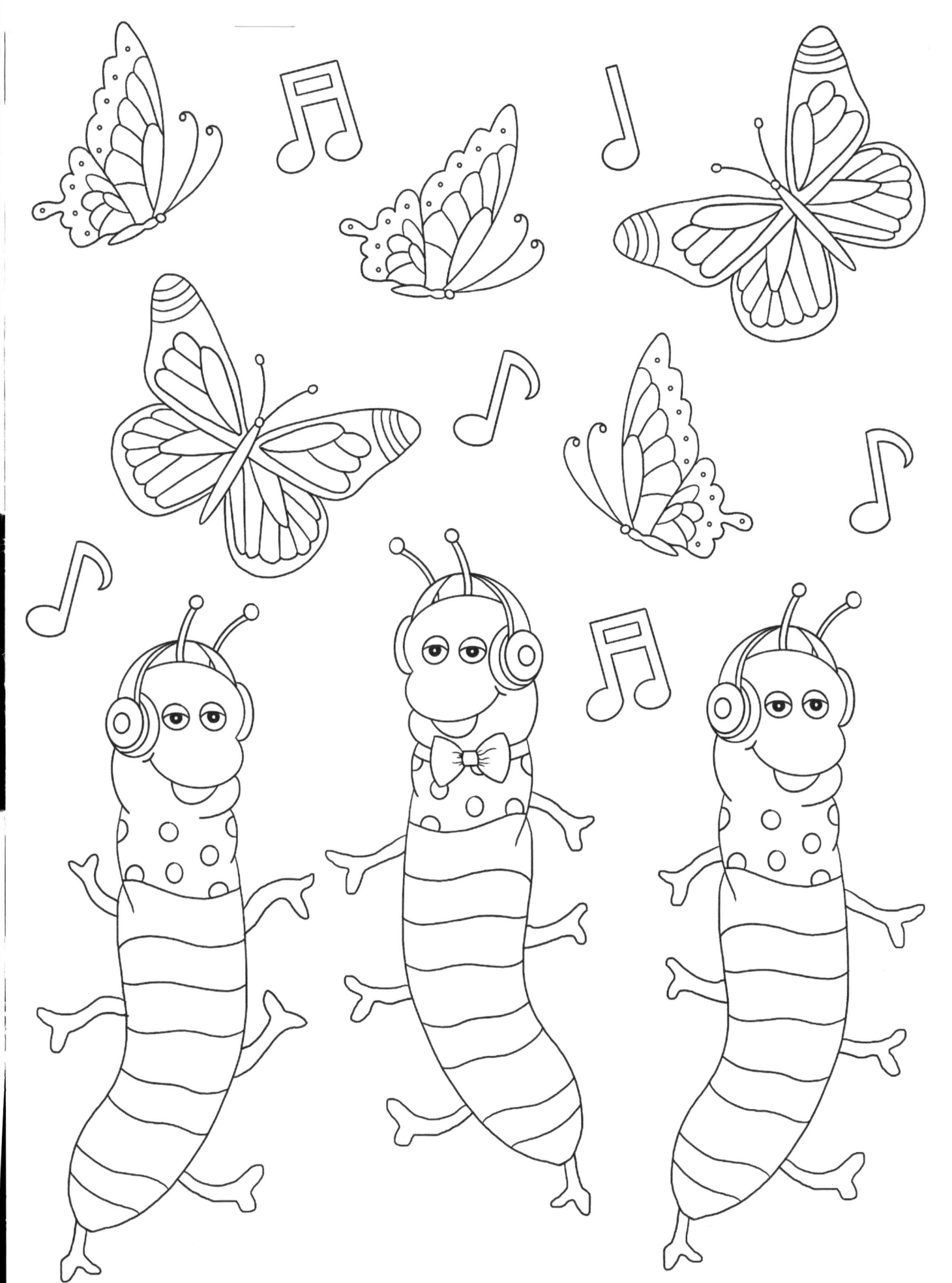

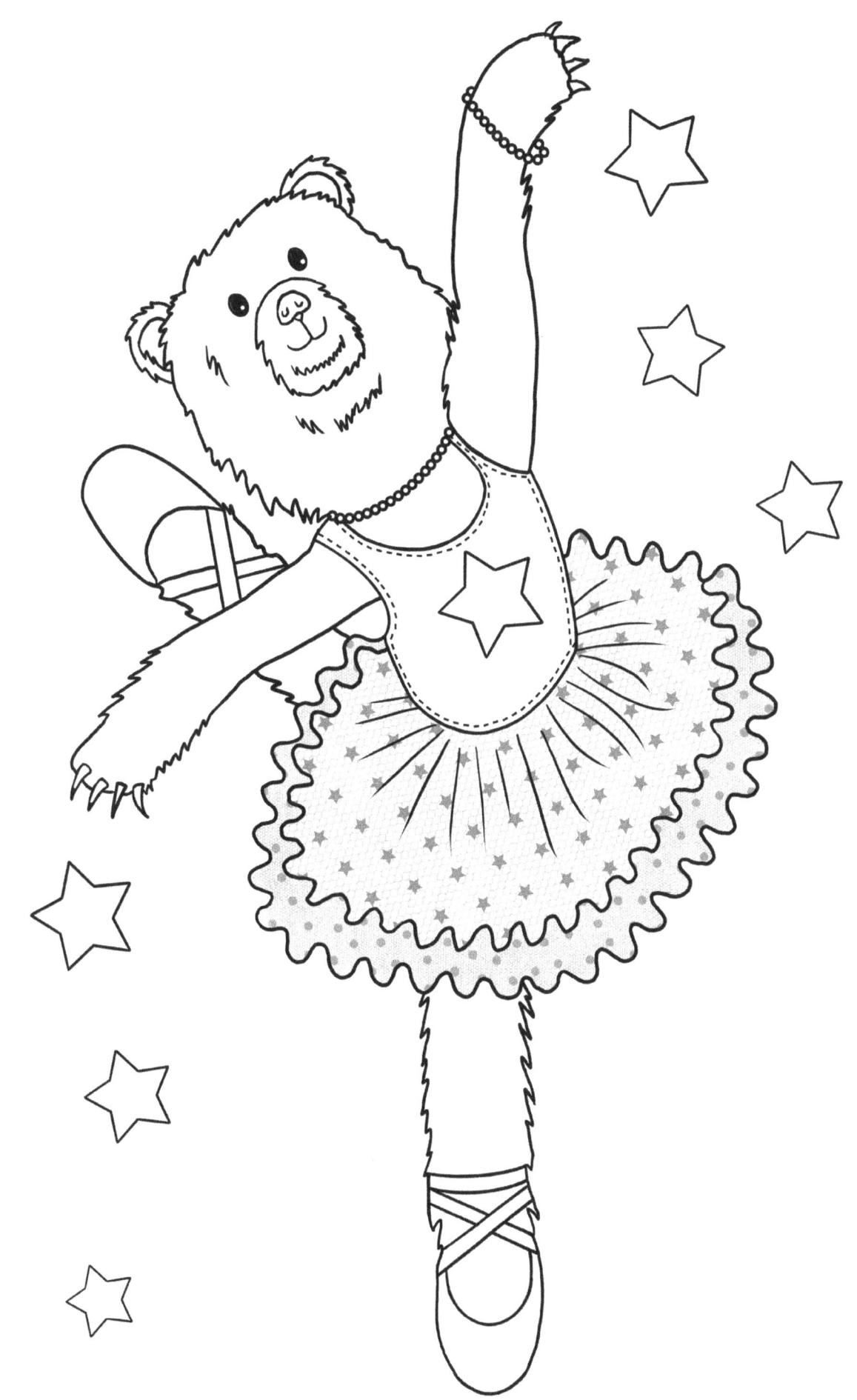

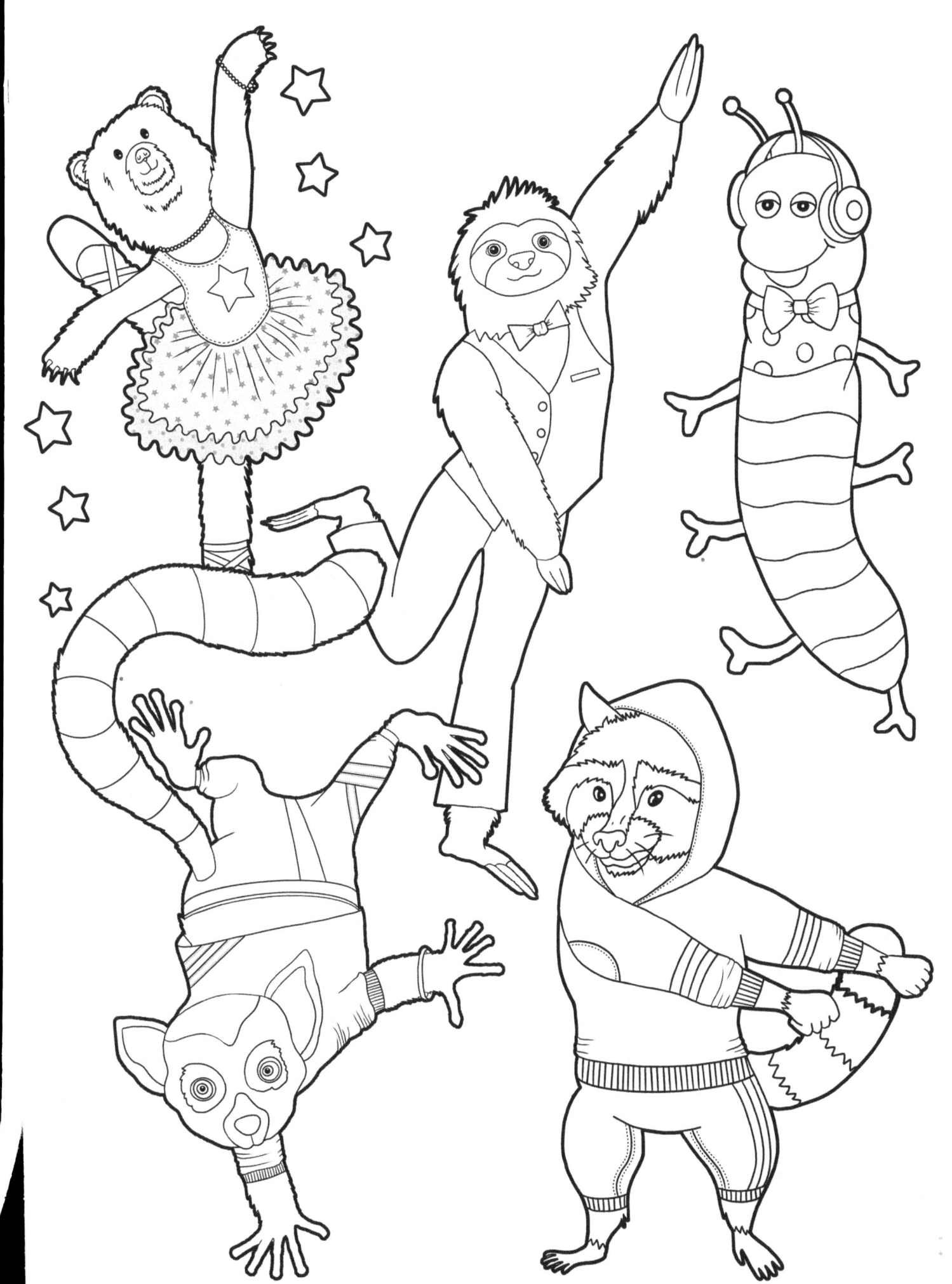

www.ingramcontent.com/pod-product-compliance
Lightning Source LLC
Chambersburg PA
CBHW080444220526
45465CB00007B/2758